Baseball

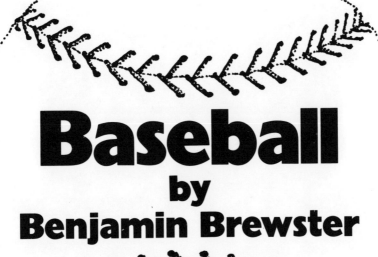

Baseball

by
Benjamin Brewster

REVISED BY BILL GUTMAN

A FIRST BOOK ● REVISED EDITION
FRANKLIN WATTS
NEW YORK ● LONDON ● 1979

Photographs courtesy of United Press International.

Library of Congress Cataloging in Publication Data

Baseball.
(A First book)
Includes index.
SUMMARY: Presents the fundamentals of baseball for
beginning players discussing the field of play, equip-
ment, rules, and basic skills and techniques.
1. Baseball—Juvenile literature.   [1. Baseball]
I. Gutman, Bill.   II. Title.
GV867.5.F64   1979   796.357   78–24230
ISBN 0–531–02932–8

Contents

Baseball

Little leaguers from Tokyo, Japan, watch
the Jeffersonville, Indiana, team as they
practice at Williamsport, Pennsylvania,
before the opening of the World Series.

Introduction

Baseball is a game for everyone. It can be played, watched, and enjoyed by boy and girl, man and woman, both old and young alike. That's why it's called the national pastime. Youngsters can begin playing baseball soon after they begin to walk. And they can play almost all their lives, anywhere there's an open field and a few others to join them. Even older people can enjoy a relaxed game of softball on a warm Sunday afternoon.

But this is a book for those just beginning to learn about and play baseball. It will teach you about the game and how to play it. It will also explain many things you can do to become a better player and talk about some of the great big-league ballplayers, both past and present.

Even though baseball is a team game, you can practice with just one or two of your friends. You can play games like one o' cat or two o' cat, or just hit grounders and flies to each other. Or you can play pitch and catch.

Sometimes you can even practice alone. The great pitcher Bob Feller used to practice when he was a boy at his parents' farm in Iowa. First he painted targets on the side of a barn. Then he threw rocks at the targets until he could pitch exactly where he wanted.

Henry Aaron, the all-time home run champ, also practiced alone. His mother once sent him out in the backyard to play with a top. But when she went outside he wasn't spinning it. He was hitting it with a baseball bat. And the Los Angeles Dodgers' all-star first baseman, Steve Garvey, practiced by hitting small, hard grapefruits that fell off the trees near his boyhood home.

There is one thing, however, that is very important. A young person must be careful when first beginning to play baseball. It is best to play with others the same age. And you should try to find some good coaches who will watch carefully and give advice. A young pitcher, for instance, should not throw too hard for too long. It is very easy to hurt your pitching arm that way.

Remember, your body is still growing and getting stronger. Pretty soon you'll be able to play all the baseball you want. And you'll be able to play for many, many years. Hopefully, this book will help you learn more about the game of baseball and will allow you to have more fun and enjoyment playing the game.

A Little About the Game

Baseball is a contest played between two teams. There are nine players on each team. The team that wins the game is the one that scores the most runs. A team scores a run when one of its players circles the bases and crosses home plate. There are four bases, including home plate. Each is 90 feet (27.4 m) apart. They form a perfect square. But when you look out from home plate, the bases make a diamond shape.

The team at bat tries to get its players around the bases. The easiest way to do this is for the batter to hit the ball so that it goes between the fielders. Sometimes a player can only run to first base. That is called a single, or one-base hit. If he goes all the way to second he has hit a double, or two-base hit. If he makes it to third it's a triple, or three-base hit. And if he can circle all the bases and cross home plate without stopping, he has hit a home run, which is also called a four-bagger, round-tripper, or circuit shot. When he stops at

"Yaz" of the Red Sox, spread-eagled,
slides safely across home plate as
Cleveland Indian catcher Roy Fosse misses the tag.

one of the bases he must then wait for the next batter to hit the ball. Then he may try to advance.

All the players on each team take turns batting. When one team is batting, the players on the other team are in the field. They are spread around the playing area in set positions, which will be discussed later. Each play starts when a player in the field called the pitcher throws the ball to home plate, where the batter is standing.

If the batter hits the ball, the players in the field try to keep him from reaching base. If the batter hits the ball in the air and a fielder catches it before it touches the ground, the batter is out. This means he cannot go to a base. He leaves the field and must wait for his next turn at bat to try again. If the batter hits the ball on the ground, one of the fielders tries to pick it up and throw to first base, where another fielder is standing. If that fielder, the first baseman, catches the ball with his foot on the base before the batter gets there, the batter is also out. But if the batter gets to the base before the ball, he is safe. He can then stay on the base.

The batter can swing at any pitch he wants. But he always looks for a good one. If he swings at a pitch but misses, it is a strike. Or if he doesn't swing at a pitch that is in the strike zone, it is also a strike. And if he hits the ball foul, it is also a strike. Three strikes and the batter is out.

On the other hand, if the batter does not swing at a pitch and it is not in the strike zone, it is called a ball. Four balls and the batter walks. That means he goes to first base and the next batter comes up.

Each team stays at bat until three players have been put out. Then the other team comes to bat. The players on that team take their turns until three are out. When both teams have had a turn at bat they have played an inning. There are nine innings in a major league game.

The Field of Play

All baseball fields are set up in the same basic way. There are strict rules for certain parts of the field. And there are also some ways in which each field is different.

Let's begin with the diamond itself, the infield. The infield is laid out the exact same way in every big-league stadium. As we said before, the diamond is a square with three bases and home plate on the corners. There are 90 feet (27.4 m) between each base. The bases are 15-inch-square (38.1-cm) white canvas bags, which are filled with a soft material and are between 3 and 5 inches (7.6 and 12.7 cm) thick. Each base is attached tightly to the ground so it won't move during a game.

Home plate is made of white rubber. It is 17 inches (43.2 cm) across, with the front end shaped like a square and the back end like a diamond. Behind the plate is an area in which the catcher must remain when the ball is being pitched.

The pitcher stands 60 feet, 6 inches (18.5 m) from home plate. This spot is marked by a 24-inch (61-cm) slab of hard,

A view from the mound.
Phillies' Larry Christenson pitching a
home run ball to Dodger Steve Garvey.

white rubber. The pitcher must always keep one foot on the rubber while delivering the ball to the batter. The rubber is in the center of a raised circle of packed dirt called the mound. The middle of the mound is some 10 inches (25.4 cm) higher than the rest of the field.

On each side of home plate there is a rectangular area known as a batter's box. These boxes are 6 feet (1.8 m) long and 4 feet (1.2 m) wide and are marked by white chalk lines before the start of each game. If a batter hits right-handed, he stands in the box on the third-base side of the plate. If he hits left-handed he stands in the box on the first-base side of the plate. Both his feet must be inside the batter's box lines as he awaits the ball from the pitcher.

There are also some other areas on the field marked by white lines. Two long lines run from home plate past first and third base and into the outfield. They are the foul lines. Balls hit on the lines or on the playing field side of the lines are fair and in play. Balls hit outside the lines away from the playing field are foul balls. They are not in play.

Both first and third base are in fair territory. They are inside the lines. The foul lines run all the way to the outfield fence. That way, fly balls and line drives can be judged fair or foul by where they land. The lines end at the outfield fence near each corner of the field. At that point there is a white pole that goes high in the air. There is one in left field and one in right field. They are called foul poles. They are used to judge whether a fly ball that passes over the fence is fair or foul.

There are also coaches' boxes outside the first and third base foul lines. They indicate where the two coaches must stand at the start of each play.

Each team has its own dugout. The dugout is a little below the level of the field and has sides and a roof. The players go down two steps to enter the dugout. They sit there when their team is at bat and watch everything that happens. The manager, coaches, and substitute players also sit in the dugout during the games. The dugouts are located between home plate and first base on one side, and home plate and third base on the other side. They are right at the beginning of the spectators' seats in foul territory.

Between the dugout and home plate on each side is a 5-foot (1.52-m) chalk circle. This is called the on deck circle. The batter who is up next kneels there waiting his turn at bat. He is said to be on deck.

Each team also has a bullpen. The bullpen is a place where a relief pitcher can warm up before coming into the game. Sometimes the bullpens are in foul territory down each line. Sometimes they are behind the outfield fence. Bullpens are never located on the field in fair territory.

Every big-league park has a large scoreboard. In the old days men used to work the scoreboard by hand. They had cards with numbers on them to show balls and strikes, the score of the game, and scores of other games. Today, most new scoreboards are huge electric ones. The scores can be changed by the push of a button. They also have message boards to keep the fans up to date on other sports and news. Some have large television screens to show "instant replays" of close calls. And some can produce colorful displays of electronic fireworks after the game or when there is a home run. All the new parks today take pride in having a fancy, modern scoreboard.

The fields have also changed. In the old days of baseball they were rough and full of rocks and pebbles. The ball could bounce any way at any time. People used to compare them with cow pastures. Later the fields became better. They had fine grass in the infield and outfield. And they had smooth dirt areas where the infielders played and around the bases. In the outfield there were dirt tracks before the outfield wall so the fielders would know they were coming close to the wall without having to look.

Today some fields are still like that. But others have what is called "artificial turf" instead of grass. Artificial turf is almost like a carpet. It is a smooth and fast surface. The only dirt area is just around the bases so players can slide.

There are even a few stadiums with huge domes on top so baseball can be played in any weather. They are even air-conditioned inside. With domed stadiums and artificial turf, some say it's almost like playing baseball in your living room.

The Equipment

A baseball is very hard, so hard that if it hits you it feels like a rock. The covering is made of two strips of white leather, which are sewn around a tightly wound ball of yarn. Inside that is a cork center, and inside that another little center of hard rubber. The official baseball weighs about 5 ounces (141.7 g) and is about 9 inches (22.9 cm) around.

Bats are made of hard wood and differ somewhat in size, weight, and design. In the very old days of baseball many bats had thick handles and actually looked like bottles. Today's bats generally have thin handles, which enable the players to snap them around quickly. Each player uses a bat that is right for him. He must feel comfortable with it and should be able to swing it easily. Don't hesitate to try another bat if things aren't going well. The pros sometimes do it when they are in slumps or late in the season when they're tired and need a lighter bat.

The catcher has more equipment than any other player.

To begin with, he must wear a mask over his face. The mask is generally made with steel bars, close enough together so the ball cannot go through. He also wears a leather chest protector to keep him from being hit there. Plastic shin guards, which go from knee to ankle, are also used for protection. And he uses a thick, rounded glove, called a catcher's mitt. It protects his hand while catching pitches thrown at nearly 100 miles (160.9 km) an hour. Baseball tradition has a name for the catcher's equipment: the "tools of ignorance."

The other players do not have nearly as much equipment. The first baseman also wears a special mitt. It is a long glove with a deep pocket so he can reach bad throws and scoop low throws out of the dirt. The other players wear gloves with fingers in them. Today's gloves are larger than those used in the past and have much deeper pockets. It is much easier to make difficult catches and to snag ground balls with today's gloves than those in the early days of the game.

Uniforms have also changed. They used to be baggy and loose and made of scratchy material. Today they are smooth, comfortable and tight-fitting. In the past the home team always wore white and the visiting team gray. Now there are many different color uniforms, some blue, some yellow, some green and gold. One team even began wearing short pants during the hot summer months a few years ago.

In addition to pants and shirt, the players also wear a brimmed cap to protect them from the sun. The fielders can wear sunglasses that flip down with a quick touch. High, tight-fitting socks are also worn to give the lower leg support and protection. Some players wear knee and hip pads to protect them when sliding. Others will wear special pads now and then to protect an injury.

Most players today also wear one or even two golf gloves when batting to protect their hands against injury. Batters must wear a special batting helmet made of hard plastic. It looks like their regular hat but will protect them if they are hit in the head with the ball.

Baseball shoes always have spikes on the bottom so the player can start and stop quickly, especially on the dirt infields. The spikes are made of metal and are very sharp. Many players have been injured by these spikes over the years. Most of the injuries happen on slides and tags. When a player is "spiked," it means he has been cut by the spikes on an opponent's shoe.

Who's Who on the Field

When one team is at bat, the nine players on the other team are in the field. The picture on page 16 shows the names and positions of the players. The first baseman, second baseman, third baseman, and shortstop are the infielders. They play in the infield near the bases. The left fielder, center fielder, and right fielder are the outfielders. They play well behind the infielders in the positions shown. The pitcher and catcher are called the battery or batterymates.

These nine players are the only ones who can catch, throw, and pick up batted balls. But they are not the only people on the field. There are also four umpires out there. It is their job to judge everything that happens on the field. One stands behind the catcher and calls the balls and strikes on each pitch. He also makes any other decisions around the plate. He wears a mask and chest protector like the catcher. There is also an umpire near each base to call the plays there.

There are also two coaches on the field. One stands in a chalk-drawn box next to first base, and the other in a box next to third. Both coaches' boxes are well in foul territory. The coaches are on the team that is batting. When that team goes into the field, the two coaches return to the dugout and the coaches from the other team come out.

The coaches' jobs are very important. They must help the team at bat, which is the offensive team. They relay instructions from the manager and also advise the players how to run the bases. All instructions are relayed by secret signals that the team works out ahead of time. Everyone on the team knows the signals.

Usually, the third-base coach gives signals to the hitter. In other words, if the manager wants the hitter to bunt, he signals the coach. The coach then signals the hitter. He may touch the tip of his cap or rub his hand across his chest. Or he may hitch his pants or clap his hands three times. Sometimes he flashes three or four signals to confuse the other team. The hitter knows which is the right one.

Coaches sometimes signal the hitter whether to swing at a certain pitch or let it go by. They also signal for plays such as the stolen base, suicide squeeze, and hit-and-run. Unless each of the players knows what to do, the play won't work. That's how important coaches are.

They also help the runners on the bases. Sometimes a coach can judge better than a runner whether the runner can make the extra base. If a player hits a ball between the outfielders, the first-base coach will wave and shout if he wants the runner to go to second. As the runner comes around second, he can look at the third-base coach, who will signal him to stop or to keep coming.

If a runner tries to score from second on a single, the

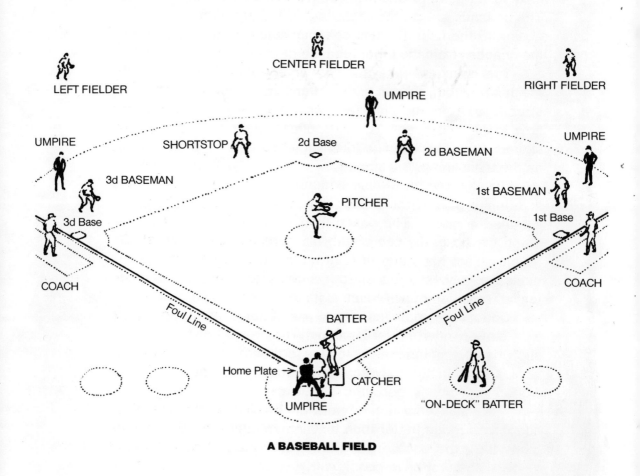

LEFT FIELDER

CENTER FIELDER

RIGHT FIELDER

UMPIRE

UMPIRE

UMPIRE

SHORTSTOP

2d Base

2d BASEMAN

3d BASEMAN

PITCHER

1st BASEMAN

3d Base

1st Base

COACH

COACH

Foul Line

Foul Line

BATTER

Home Plate →

CATCHER

UMPIRE

"ON-DECK" BATTER

A BASEBALL FIELD

third-base coach will either hold up his hands for the runner to stop at third or wave him through like a traffic cop. If a throw is coming into third at the same time as the runner, the coach can signal for the runner to slide or to come in standing up. Of course, the players must keep their eyes open, too. But it's a big help to have a couple of good coaches out there.

The man who runs the team on the field is the manager. Some managers used to coach third base. Now most of them sit in the dugout during the game. They signal the coaches from there. They also talk to the players, tell the outfielders where to play, and make all of the decisions during a game.

Sometimes a manager won't come onto the field once during a game. Other times he comes out during an inning to change pitchers or maybe to argue a call with an umpire. In the old days many managers also played. Greats like Ty Cobb, Tris Speaker, and Rogers Hornsby were all playing managers at one time. But it isn't easy being a player and a manager. It isn't done much anymore. The last one to try it was Frank Robinson with the Cleveland Indians in the mid 1970s. But he only did it for one year. The next year he retired as a player and was just a manager.

A manager has more things to think about than anyone else on a team. It's a very hard job in today's game.

During a ball game, the team that's playing in its own stadium (called the home team) goes out onto the field first. The visiting team is always the first to come to bat. So they always bat in the top of an inning, while the home team bats in the bottom of the inning.

These are the things you will see happening on the field during each game. Now we'll take a closer look at the game itself to see what each player must do if he wants to play well.

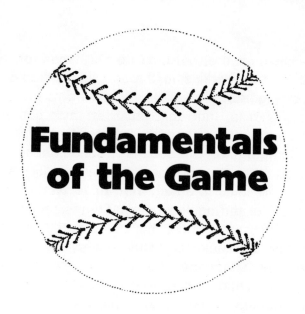

Fundamentals of the Game

● BATTING

At first glance, hitting a baseball may look very easy. After all, a player just gets up there, swings the bat, and BANG! Unless, of course, he misses. And that can happen very easily. In fact, there are many people who think that hitting a baseball well may be the most difficult skill in all of sports.

Every great hitter in the history of baseball has practiced, practiced, practiced. Players like Ty Cobb, Ted Williams, and Rod Carew have always said you can't get enough batting practice. Their advice is practice all you can, then practice some more.

Of course, good offensive baseball is more than just hitting the ball. Every hit can't be a home run. But since each play begins with the pitcher throwing the ball toward the batter, hitting is where it all begins. And as you will learn, there are many things a batter can do to help his team.

When he's at the plate, a batter must think about one thing—his hitting. He has just a split second to look at the pitch, decide whether he likes it, and swing at it. He must concentrate so his actions are almost automatic. He must also be ready to hold up and let a pitch go past him. So every single pitch requires a split-second decision.

If the batter lets a pitch go past that is in the strike zone, the umpire will call it a strike. The strike zone is that space over home plate and between the batter's armpits and top of his knees when he takes his natural stance. Any pitch higher or lower than the zone or not over the plate on either side is a ball. Some pitches are very close. Sometimes a batter will swing "to protect the plate." That means he isn't sure whether it will be a strike or a ball. If he has two strikes, he must often do this. If he doesn't swing, the umpire must make a hard but quick decision, or call.

There are more things that the batter must watch for besides where the pitch is coming. He has to watch for the kind of pitch that is thrown and the speed at which it is coming. For the pitcher is always trying to fool him. He may throw many kinds of pitches. Some come in straight and fast. Others curve. Still others come in slower or "off speed." Most pitchers try to throw all these pitches with the same arm motion. So the batter must be very alert. We will talk more about the different kinds of pitches later.

The batter must watch out for one other thing. Every now and then a ball will get away from the pitcher. It will not go anywhere near where he wants it. Sometimes it goes right at the batter. So the batter must be ready to duck or get out of the way. He can be badly hurt if hit by a pitched ball. Batters have suffered broken wrists or arms when hit by pitches. Others have received serious head injuries. If a batter is hit, even slightly, he goes to first base and the next batter comes up.

● HOW TO HIT THE BALL

Perhaps you have wondered why a batter sometimes hits the ball high in the air, other times on the ground, and still other times on a straight line? And why does he hit it in one direction his first time up and the opposite way his next time up? The answer is in the way he has swung at the ball and how the bat makes contact with the ball.

To make good contact, a batter must be comfortable at the plate. He must find a good batting stance for himself. This is the way he stands in the batter's box waiting for the pitch. Most players, both right- and left-handed batters, stand with their feet spread apart somewhat. They bend or crouch a bit at the knees so they'll be able to move quickly. And they keep their bat high and away from their bodies so they won't get tangled up when they swing.

There is no one correct batting stance. Each hitter has his own. In fact, some big leaguers have had some very strange batting stances. For years, people wondered how Stan Musial could hit a baseball from his stance. His feet were tight together. He crouched so low he looked like he was sitting in a chair. He held his bat high over his head and turned his head at a strange angle toward the pitcher. People laughed at first. But Musial became one of the greatest hitters in baseball history. He played for more than twenty years and never changed his stance once. The point is, young players must find the stance that is right and comfortable for them.

Young hitters should work to develop a level swing. That means the bat should move parallel to the ground as it meets the ball. If the center of the bat meets the center of the ball, the ball should travel straight and fast. This kind of hit is called a line drive.

If the bat hits below the center of the ball, the ball will go up into the air. If it's hit just a little below the center, the ball can go a long way. This is a fly ball. A fly ball going over the outfield fence is a home run. But if the bat hits too far below the center of the ball, the ball will go way up in the air, but not travel very far. This is called a pop-up or pop fly. If the ball does not go very high, it's sometimes called a blooper. And if it falls in between the infielders and out-fielders, it's called a Texas Leaguer, or Texas League single.

On the other hand, if the bat hits above the center of the ball, the ball will go downward and bounce along the ground. This, of course, is called a bouncer or grounder. Sometimes a ball is hit very hard and goes along the ground without bouncing. That's called a grasscutter.

As players grow older, they sometimes change their swing. Men with great power who can hit many home runs will sometimes swing up or uppercut the ball. They feel they have a better chance of hitting home runs that way. And some hitters with good running speed and not much power feel they have a better chance if they hit the ball on the ground. So they sometimes swing down or chop at the ball. But it's best to start with a good, level swing. Then you can change it as you get older if you feel it's best for you.

When a batter swings at a pitch is also very important. If he swings and connects just as the ball is going past him, he will hit it right back up the middle of the field. If he swings a bit too soon, he will "pull" the ball. This means, if he's a right-handed hitter, that he'll pull the ball to left field. And if he's a left-handed hitter, he'll pull it to right.

On the other hand, if he swings a bit later, the ball will go the other way. The right-handed hitter will hit to right field, and the left-handed hitter to left field. This is called hitting to the opposite field. If the batter swings very early or very late, then he will hit the ball into foul territory. A foul counts as a strike, but a player cannot strike out on a foul ball. With two strikes on him, a foul means nothing. The batter has another chance to hit the ball.

Sometimes a batter tries to hit early or late on purpose. The outfield fences are always closer to the plate in left and right field than in center. Home run hitters usually try to pull the ball and hit it in the air. The great Babe Ruth was a left-handed pull hitter, while Hank Aaron was a right-handed pull hitter.

Hitters who try to place the ball in a certain spot will also swing early or late on purpose. Sometimes they'll swing at an outside pitch and try to hit it to the opposite field. That's called going with the pitch. Other times they'll try to aim the ball between the fielders. Home run hitters usually hold the bat as far down on the handle as they can. Place hitters hold their hands farther up the bat. A small portion of the bat sticks out from below their hands. This is called choking up on the bat.

Left: Pete Rose begins his swing as the pitch flies toward the plate. He connected for his forty-fourth consecutive game hit. Right: one of the great batters of today—Rod Carew—completes a full swing.

Of course, a batter doesn't get on base every time he hits the ball. There are many ways he can make an out. A good hitter is one who can keep his average at .300. This means he gets three hits for every ten times at bat. So he also makes seven outs. You can see it's not easy to get a hit. The fielders can catch flies and line drives before they hit the ground. And the infielders can pick up grounders and throw the ball to first before the batter gets there. Or the batter can strike out. Those are the most common ways batters are put out.

The hardest thing for a batter happens when he goes into a "slump." A slump is when he just can't seem to get any hits, no matter what he does. It's hard to explain why a slump happens. Sometimes the batter begins swinging a little differently from usual. Or he holds the bat differently. Sometimes he starts trying too hard. The only way to break a slump is to work harder. Take extra practice and just try to "meet" the ball easily when you're up. To meet the ball means to strive to hit the center of the ball with the center of the bat.

● BUNTING

Bunting is a very important part of baseball. A good bunter is a valuable player to have on the team. The manager and coaches like all their players to be able to bunt well, for there are certain times when all players are called upon to bunt the ball.

When a player is going to bunt, he slides his top hand about halfway up the bat and turns to face the pitcher. He holds the bat very loosely and doesn't swing at the ball. Instead, he lets the ball simply hit the bat and bounce off. The ball will not go very far. If the bunt is made correctly, the ball will roll between 10 and 20 feet (3.05 and 6.1 m) from the plate.

However, bunts should be aimed just like hits. Players should try not to bunt straight in front of the plate. The pitcher or catcher can field those too quickly. Instead, they should try to bunt down the foul lines, which makes the ball harder to field. The batter should also not "square around" to bunt too quickly. He should try to hide his plan as long as he can, because once he is in the bunting position, all the fielders charge in quickly to get the ball.

The most common kind of bunt is the sacrifice bunt. This happens when there is a runner on first base, or runners on first and second. The batter bunts hoping the runner or runners can move up to the next base. This will make it easier for them to score. The batter hopes the fielder will throw it to first. And if he makes a good bunt, that's the only play the fielder can make. Of course, the batter would also like to beat the throw himself for a hit. But on a sacrifice, the batter is usually thrown out. Thus he's sacrificing himself for the good of the team. A sacrifice bunt does not count as a time at bat on the batter's record. Players try to sacrifice only with none or one out, never with two out.

The bunt is also used on a squeeze play. A squeeze play can only be used when there is a runner on third base. On the suicide squeeze the runner breaks for home when the ball is pitched. If the batter bunts the ball safely, the runner usually makes it. If the batter misses the bunt, the runner will usually be thrown out.

The safety squeeze is a bit different. The runner waits to see where the batter bunts. If it's a good bunt that can't be fielded quickly, the runner breaks for home and tries to make it. The squeeze play is used to take the fielders by surprise. So everyone on the field must think and act quickly with no hesitation.

A player may also bunt for a hit. He usually does this

with no one on base. Once again he is trying to take the defense by surprise. So he doesn't show the bunting position until the last possible second. And he begins running hard toward first as soon as he bunts the ball. There's nothing wrong with bunting for a base hit. Rod Carew practices his bunting every day and has had as many as twenty-five bunt hits a year. That can really help your batting average.

The left-handed batter has an advantage when bunting for a hit. He is closer to first base and can get there faster. Some lefties try what is called a drag bunt. It is a longer bunt that the batter tries to push past the pitcher and between the first and second baseman. If done right, the drag bunt is almost a sure hit. One of the best drag bunters was Mickey Mantle. Mantle was a great home run hitter. But every now and then he'd surprise everyone with a drag bunt. So everyone should learn how to bunt, even the big, strong power hitters.

● BASERUNNING

Up to now, we've talked about hitters and all the things they do to get on base. Once they are on base, they must use another set of baseball skills. That is baserunning.

There's a lot more to baserunning than just going as fast as you can. Speed helps, of course. But a runner must know what to do and when to do it. It's not easy to become a really good base runner. Like everything else, it takes a good deal of practice and knowledge of the game.

Even simply running around the bases takes practice. Since first, second, and third base all stick up above the

Yankee Reggie Jackson, the power hitter, rarely bunts but this time he must—to move a base runner along.

ground, a poor base runner can trip over the bags. The good runner knows just how to hit each base. He hits it on the corner with his foot and then pushes off toward the next base. He must also make his turns sharp and neat. If he turns too wide, he'll lose time going to the next base. The runner must also be careful to touch every base. If he misses one, a fielder can tag the base with the ball and the runner is out.

The runner must also stay in the base lines when he's running. He can't dodge in and out or run wide to avoid a tag. The base lines are straight lines between each base. They aren't marked between first and second base or second and third base, but the umpire will judge whether or not a player runs out of the base line.

When a batter is running to first, he is allowed to run beyond the base and not be tagged out, unless he misses the bag. When he stops he can turn and walk back to the base. But if he turns and makes an attempt to run toward second, the first baseman can try to tag him out. At second and third, a runner must be more careful. There, he is safe only if he keeps his foot or hand on the bag. The runner is out if a fielder touches him with the ball while he is off base.

Running the bases is often a matter of quick starts and stops. This is also something a runner can practice and improve. But the best way to get into a base on a close play is to slide. There are several ways to slide into a base. These, too, take a lot of practice.

There is the straight in, or pop-up, slide. This one is used by the all-time base-stealing king, Lou Brock. The runner goes straight at the base full speed. When he is close enough he starts his slide. He puts one leg out in front, the other folded under it, bent at the knee. When his front foot hits the bag he uses the folded leg to push himself right up on his feet. Thus, the pop-up slide.

Then there is the hook slide. This is where the runner slides to one side of the base and hooks the bag with his trailing leg. The trailing leg is bent to the outside of his body. This slide is harder on the body than the pop-up. The fall-away slide is similar. The runner goes straight in and at the last second falls away to one side or the other, trying to avoid the tag. Again he hooks the bag with his leg, and even sometimes with his hand. Great base stealers like Ty Cobb and Maury Wills used hook and fall-away slides.

The final kind of slide is the most simple. It is the head-first slide. The runner simply throws his body or leaps at the base headfirst. This slide is very exciting but can be dangerous. Your body can take a beating on the chest and stomach. You can get tagged or even kicked in the head. One player who always slides headfirst is Pete Rose. And he's one of the most exciting players in the game.

There are a few other things a player must learn about baserunning. He must know how fast he can get from base to base. That way he can decide whether to try for the extra base or not. This also means knowing how good a throwing arm the fielder has. It's harder to take the extra base on a fielder with a strong arm.

If a player is on base and a long fly ball is hit, he can try for the next base only after the ball is caught. This is called "tagging up." When the ball is hit, he returns to the base and waits. He cannot leave until the ball is in the fielder's glove. Then he must start as fast as he can and go as hard as he can to the next base. Many runs are scored when players on third tag up on a fly ball and come home. This is done the most often because it requires the longest throw for the outfielder. A player scoring this way has scored on a sacrifice fly. The batter is not charged with a time at bat, but he gets a run batted in.

● STEALING

Stealing a base takes another special skill. The good base stealers are usually fast runners. But the best ones combine speed with several other things. A stolen base occurs when a runner breaks toward the next base as the pitcher delivers the ball and the runner beats the throw to that base by the catcher.

That means, of course, that the batter does not hit the ball on that play. If he hits the ball or even fouls it off, there cannot be a stolen base on that pitch. However, if he swings and misses and the runner makes it safely, it is a stolen base. The way a runner is caught stealing is when he's tagged out by one of the fielders before safely reaching the base.

You can steal second, third, or home. Most steals are of second base. Third is more difficult to steal because it's a shorter throw for the catcher. A steal of home is very unusual.

To steal a base a player must be very alert. He must know just how the pitcher moves. Then he can start running the split second he knows the pitcher will throw toward the plate. If he runs too soon, the pitcher can throw to the base and catch the man in a rundown. If he starts too late, the catcher will throw him out easily.

Top: it looks as though Jose Cruz of the Houston Astros will be tagged out at the plate by Gene Tenace of the San Diego Padres—but he made it. Bottom: one of the great base stealers of all time, the St. Louis Cardinals' Lou Brock, shows how it should be done.

The runner must also take the biggest lead that he can. That means he must get as far off the base as possible so that he is closer to the base he is trying to steal. But if he gets too far off the base, the pitcher can throw over and he can be tagged out. If the pitcher throws over, the runner must get back to the base quickly.

He must also know how to slide well. We talked about that in the last section.

Great base stealers like Ty Cobb, Jackie Robinson, Maury Wills, and Lou Brock watched every move on the baseball field. They knew each pitcher and catcher. They practiced and worked hard so they would have every advantage. And they made the pitchers worry about them stealing. That can even help the batter. But that's the only way you can be a great base stealer.

● BATTING ORDER

Before every game, the manager of each team writes out the order in which the players on his team will bat. He then gives it to the plate umpire. This batting order cannot be changed during a game. The only change can be a substitution. That's when one player who hasn't been in the game yet takes the place of another at bat. He is called a pinch hitter. And the player taken out of the game cannot return.

There is one exception to this. For the past several years, the American League has had a designated hitter. He is a player who hits instead of the pitcher. He does not play in the field and comes to bat only when it's the pitcher's turn. The pitcher never bats, but can stay in the game to pitch. In the National League, there is no designated hitter rule. The pitcher bats for himself. And if he is replaced by a pinch hitter, he must leave the game.

The Positions

● THE PITCHER

Many people feel the pitcher has the hardest job on the team. After all, he's got to start every single play by throwing the ball to home plate. And he has got to throw it hard and with great accuracy. He cannot relax or let up. A mistake could cost his team a ball game, especially if the score is close.

The pitcher must be strong and in excellent physical condition. He must take good care of his arm. But he must also keep his legs in shape. If his legs get tired, he won't pitch right, no matter how strong his arm feels.

Besides pitching, the pitcher must be ready to act as an infielder if the batter hits the ball toward him. He must also watch the base runners to keep them from stealing. Sometimes he must run behind first, third, or home if there is a throw coming there. His job is to catch the ball if his teammate misses it. This is called backing up a play.

During a game, a pitcher will throw many pitches. And he must throw each one with one foot on the pitcher's rubber. This cannot change. If he steps off the rubber before delivering the ball, play is delayed until he gets back on. That's when he's ready again.

He must also know how to throw several kinds of pitches and how to change speeds and pitch to different spots on the plate. This will keep the hitter off balance. He won't know what is coming next or where it is coming to.

The most basic pitch is the fastball. This is a ball thrown hard and straight. Though no two pitchers throw exactly alike, most hold the ball between their thumb and first two fingers when they want to throw the fastball. They let it go straight out of their hand. Some pitchers throw directly overhand. Others throw three-quarters overhand, and still others sidearm. But the ball is held and released the same way for the fastball. Though it is supposed to be a straight pitch, some fastballs move or hop. This is due to several things. It can be how the pitcher throws it, how fast it travels, or how the rotation of the ball acts on the air currents. A hop on a fastball seems to be a natural thing. Some pitchers have it, some don't.

The curveball is not natural. It is a pitch thrown a special way. The rotation of the ball and the air currents combine to make the ball actually curve as it comes to the plate. The ball is held like a fastball. But as the pitcher is about to release it, he snaps his wrist and allows the ball to roll over his first finger.

Steve Carlton of the Phillies
starts his windup as he
prepares to work the batter.

When a right-handed pitcher throws the curve, the ball curves or breaks away from a right-handed hitter. With a left-handed pitcher it is just the opposite. The curve is also a slower pitch than a fastball. Many pitchers today throw what is called a slider. It is really a fast curve. In other words, it is thrown the same way as a curve, but harder. So it doesn't break as much, but the break is quicker. To many pitchers, a good slider is a better pitch than a curve.

A screwball is really a reverse curve. But not nearly as many pitchers throw it. That's because it is thrown with a more unnatural motion. If a pitcher isn't careful, he can hurt his arm or elbow throwing the screwball. As the pitcher releases the ball, he snaps his wrist in, letting the ball roll off his second finger. It's harder to snap the wrist this way. Just try it without a ball and you'll see. But when a right-handed pitcher throws a screwball, the ball breaks in on a right-handed hitter and away from a left-handed hitter.

Another uncommon pitch is called the knuckleball. It is a difficult pitch to master. That's because it is hard to control. But a pitcher with a good knuckleball can drive batters crazy. Sometimes he even drives his own catcher crazy. That's because it's hard to predict just where a knuckleball will go. It darts and dances all over the place. Sometimes, in fact, it's called a flutterball.

The knuckleball is held differently from the other pitches. Instead of gripping the ball with the first two fingers, most knuckleball pitchers dig their two fingernails into the ball. It isn't really held with the knuckles as many people think. The pitcher then pushes the ball straight toward the plate. He releases it in such a way that the ball doesn't rotate. With no rotation, the ball seems to catch the different air currents and may move several ways before reaching the plate. Or it may fall away at the last minute.

A good knuckleball is hard to hit and hard to catch. Most catchers use a slightly larger mitt when catching a knuckleball pitcher. The knuckleball is thrown easily and puts very little strain on the arm. One of the most famous knuckleball pitchers of all time was Hoyt Wilhelm. Because he threw almost all knucklers, he stayed in the majors until he was forty-nine years old. Still, the knuckler is a hard pitch to master. Sometimes it takes years to develop.

There are also some trick pitches that were used in the old days but are against the rules today. One is the spitball. It's just what it sounds like. The pitcher wets the ball before he throws it. For some reason, the wetness makes the ball move quickly. Many spitballs drop away at the last second. This makes them very hard to hit. It is thought that some pitchers today try to sneak in a spitball once in a while. But if they are caught they are penalized.

The old-timers used other tricks. Sometimes they would cut the ball with a sharp metal object. Other times they would rub grease or something else on it. Anything that is done to a baseball makes it act differently. So today none of those things are allowed.

With all pitches, it is a general rule that it is better to keep the ball low. Pitchers like to shoot for the low part of the strike zone. Not with every single pitch, perhaps, but with a good many of them. Low or sinking pitches are usually hit on the ground, giving the infielders a good chance to throw the batter out. A high pitch is more likely to be hit in the air. Very few home runs are hit off low and sinking pitches.

It is the catcher who usually tells the pitcher what to throw—fastball, curve, and so on. He is more aware of the hitters and of what pitches are working well that day. He signals the pitcher with his fingers, and hides the signals down between his legs when he squats. The simplest signals are one finger for a fastball, two fingers for a curve, three for a change of pace. A change of pace is when a pitcher fakes a fastball and throws it slower instead.

If the pitcher doesn't want to throw a certain pitch he shakes his head. The catcher will then give him another signal. The pitcher must take all signals with his foot on the rubber. He hides the ball in his glove and gets ready for his windup. He hides the ball so the batter can't see him adjust his grip for a certain kind of pitch.

The pitcher uses a windup only if there are no runners on base. In the windup, a pitcher swings his arms over his head before kicking his front leg up and pitching. The windup gives most pitchers better rhythm and sometimes more speed on the ball.

However, if there is a runner on first, or on first and second, they can easily steal a base if the pitcher winds up. So with runners on, he comes to what is called a stop or set position. He stands sideways to the plate, brings his arms over his head, then stops at his belt for a second. He then looks at the runner to make sure he is not too far off the base. If he is, the pitcher can throw over. If the runner is not too far off, the pitcher kicks and throws to the plate.

Top: Yankee power-pitcher Ron Guidry shows us his long stretch before making the delivery. Bottom: the ball is fired away by Guidry. It is probably traveling nearly 100 miles (160.9 km) an hour.

Once the pitcher starts toward the plate he cannot stop and throw to a base. If he does, a balk is called. The runner or runners are then allowed to move up one base.

With a runner on third, second and third, or with the bases loaded, a pitcher will likely take his full windup. That's because home is so difficult to steal that the runner isn't likely to try it. If there is a really good base runner on third, the pitcher might decide to use his set position. It's up to him.

If a pitcher goes the full nine innings, he has pitched a complete game. But if the other team is hitting him well, or he is tired or hurt, another pitcher must come in. This man is called a relief pitcher. A manager can use as many relief pitchers as he wants during a game. Also, if a pinch hitter goes up for the pitcher, a relief pitcher must come in.

Sometimes a manager will make a change because of the batters coming up. In general, it is harder for a right-handed hitter to hit a right-handed pitcher, and harder for a left-handed hitter to hit a left-handed pitcher. So if a good left-handed hitter is coming up against a right-handed pitcher in an important spot, the manager might bring a left-handed pitcher into the game. The feeling is that he would have a better chance of getting the hitter out. Of course, the top hitters can hit against anyone. And the best pitchers can get anyone out. Still, there is a lot of lefty-righty switching done in the majors today.

All pitchers must warm up before they enter a game. If they threw hard without warm-ups they might hurt their arms. Starting pitchers warm up for fifteen or twenty minutes before the game. And relief pitchers warm up in the bullpen if they think they might be needed.

Pitching is very hard on the arm. That's why starting pitchers must have three, four, or even five days rest between starts. Relievers can pitch more often. But that's because they only pitch one or two innings at a time. Some pitchers have to soak their arms in ice after the game to keep any swelling down.

So pitching isn't easy. It takes work and practice, and pitchers must take very good care of their bodies. No wonder top pitchers are hard to find. But a team can't win without them. There is an old baseball saying that good pitching will stop good hitting anytime. And that is true. A good pitcher will never have trouble finding a job in the major leagues.

● THE CATCHER

The catcher must be a strong and durable player. He takes more of a physical beating than any other player on the field. For one thing, he must squat down and get up hundreds of times a game. This is very hard on the legs. Many catchers lose running speed after several years because of the squatting.

Secondly, the catcher is a prime target for getting hit with foul balls. Even though he wears a mask, chest protector, and shin guards, he is often hit. In the old days, catchers were always splitting and breaking fingers on their bare hand. Today's catchers have better gloves and many of them catch one-handed. They keep their bare hand out of the way until they have caught the pitch.

Catchers are also prime targets on plays at the plate. When a runner is trying to score, the catcher will go up the third-base line a few feet and wait for the throw. What he is doing is called blocking the plate. The runner can then try to run him down, knock him over, or slide into him. Since the runner is moving and the catcher is standing still, it is the catcher who gets the worst of these collisions. And if he

During the 1978 All Star game Cincinnati's
George Foster scores as Oriole pitcher
Jim Palmer backs up Bosox catcher Carlton Fisk.

drops the ball, the runner will be safe. So he's got to hold onto it no matter how hard he is hit. This comes with the job and all catchers know it. But that doesn't make it any easier.

In addition to being tough, the catcher must be smart. As we said before, he must call the game for the pitcher. He must also know just what is happening on the field and instruct the other players what to watch for. Plus he has to know when his pitcher is getting tired. Then he can tell the manager whether to take him out for a relief pitcher or leave him in. So the catcher has a great deal of responsibility. And when he comes up to bat he's got to forget all this and just think about his hitting. Otherwise, he won't hit.

When a runner tries to steal a base, it is the catcher who must try to throw him out. The distance from home to second is a shade over 127 feet (38.7 m). That's a long throw. And the catcher must throw quickly and hard, keeping the ball low to the ground. And he must do it by springing quickly out of his crouch. So with everything else, the catcher must have a quick and powerful arm.

He must also be quick enough to spring out from behind the plate to field bunts. And he's got to be able to go back to catch high foul pops. Sometimes these are hit almost straight up in the air and are among the hardest kinds of flies to catch.

Because of all this, it is no wonder that there have not been too many superstar catchers down through the years. In the old days there were players like Gabby Hartnett, Mickey Cochrane, and Bill Dickey. Then there was Yogi Berra and Roy Campanella. Today you have Johnny Bench, Thurman Munson, Ted Simmons, and Carlton Fisk. They're all great players and great catchers. But there really haven't been too many really great ones. It's a tough position.

● FIRST BASEMAN

First base is a busy position. The first baseman must take many throws from his infielders during the course of a game. Some of them may be high, some low, some in the dirt. He's got to know how to get them before the runner crosses the bag.

The first baseman must have one foot on the base when he takes the throw in order to put the runner out. Therefore, he must know how to move his feet. He must judge where the throw is coming and put the proper foot on the bag. Then he reaches out as far as he can for the throw. This is called stretching for the throw. First basemen stretch so that they will get the ball a split second sooner. Sometimes a play is so close at first that a stretch can make the difference.

For that reason many baseball people prefer tall players at first base. A player like Willie "Stretch" McCovey of the Giants is a typical example. McCovey is 6 feet, 4 inches (1.9 m) tall. When he plays first it seems that he can reach for the sky for a throw or stretch halfway to short or third. He is a fine fielding first sacker.

But shorter players can play the position, too. Steve Garvey of the Los Angeles Dodgers may be the best fielding first baseman in the game today. Yet he is only 5 feet, 10 inches (1.7 m) tall. But Garvey can do everything well. Maybe he can't reach as high as some taller players. But he has learned how to make up for it. He is extremely good at leaping for high throws and in one motion sweeping his glove back and tagging the runner before he crosses the bag. So you don't have to be a giant to play first. You've just got to work hard at it.

Left-handers have a slight advantage playing first. Their glove is on their right hand. This gives them an edge in pick-

**Larry Lintz of the Montreal Expos
races back to first to avoid
a pickoff as Steve Garvey of the
Dodgers waits for the ball.**

ing up balls hit to their right. They also have an easier throw to other bases since they don't have to shift their feet as would a righty thrower.

The first baseman doesn't always play on the base. With no one on first, he plays several feet off the bag. This way he can go to his right for grounders and still cover the ground to his left between himself and the foul line. And, of course, he can get over to the bag in plenty of time to take a throw from his infielders.

When there is a runner on the base, the first baseman will hold him on. He stands with one foot on the base and holds his glove up so that the pitcher will have a target to throw to. This keeps the runner closer and makes it harder for him to steal.

● SECOND BASEMAN

The second baseman is generally a smaller player, but one who is very quick. He stands between first and second in the infield. He has to have the speed and quickness to move in either direction and to cover either base. And he must also have a quick arm, though it doesn't have to be as strong as the shortstop's or third baseman's. The second baseman doesn't have to make as long a throw as they normally do.

The second baseman must know how to tag out runners on steal attempts. Either the second baseman or shortstop covers second base on a steal. So the second sacker must be ready to deal with a base runner who is sliding into him at full speed.

He must also know how to make the double play. This occurs when there is a runner on first and a grounder is hit

**Rod Carew leaps high in the air to
avoid a sliding Bert Campaneris
after releasing the ball to begin a double play.**

to the infield. If it's hit to short or third, the second baseman runs to second to take the throw. If it beats the runner, he is forced out and the second baseman then throws to first to try to beat the runner there. If his throw is on time, it is a double play. Both runners are out on one play.

This is not easy. The infielders must work together and their timing must be just right. The second baseman should get the ball just as he moves across the bag. He must then pivot and throw to first. However, the runner's job is to take the second baseman out of the play. So the runner often goes after the fielder. The second baseman must be agile enough to jump over the sliding runner and throw while in the air. Otherwise, he can be spiked.

Like the other fielders, the second baseman needs all the skills. He must be able to go back and catch pop-ups, run in for slow grounders, and throw off balance. And he's got to know when to run out to the outfield for relay throws.

● THE SHORTSTOP

Like the second baseman, the shortstop must be fast on his feet. He must cover a lot of ground. That's called having good range. He normally plays between second and third base. But he must often run all the way behind second for grounders or go deep into the third-base, shortstop hole. Going into the hole is one of the toughest plays for a short-stop. He moves back and to his right and usually grabs the ball backhanded. He then must stop quickly and make a long but strong throw to first. This one play can take years of practice to get right.

The shortstop must also be ready to tag runners on steal attempts and work the double play. He doesn't have to pivot and watch for runners on the DP like the second baseman.

He's usually moving across the bag and can throw without first making a pivot. But unless the timing between the two infielders is right, he can also be hit hard by the runner coming in.

Also like the second sacker, the shortstop must be able to go out for pop flies. He must often run behind the third baseman and catch pops in foul territory. And he's got to know how to take relay throws from the outfield and quickly throw to the right base. It's been said that no team can really win without a good shortstop.

The shortstop and second baseman are often referred to as the team's keystone combination, or keystone combo.

● THIRD BASEMAN

The third baseman doesn't have to handle as many balls as the other infielders do. In many cases, he is not as fast as the second baseman and shortstop. But he must have a powerful throwing arm and a very quick glove. That's because many balls are hit at him at very great speed. That's why third is often called the hot corner.

The third baseman generally plays several feet off the third base foul line. How far depends on the hitter. He always tries to guard the line. In other words, he tries to keep batted balls from getting between him and the third-base bag. If they do, it's usually at least a double. That's why you see so many third basemen diving for balls hit down the line. Players like Brooks Robinson and Graig Nettles have made many of these diving plays. Often they catch the ball on one or two bounces, but are lying flat on their stomachs. So they must get up very quickly and throw to first. Sometimes they must throw from their knees or sitting down. And sometimes they must run in very quickly for bunts and slow rollers, and throw off balance. That's why the third baseman needs a strong arm.

Sometimes the third baseman has to cut in front of the shortstop for slow hoppers because he can get there faster and is in better position for the throw. He must also know how to make tag plays and go back for pops.

Like the shortstop and second baseman, the third baseman always throws right-handed. A lefty thrower could not play any of those three infield positions because he would always be out of position for the throw.

● THE OUTFIELDERS

An outfielder might not be as busy as an infielder, but his job is just as important. And he's often in the action when the game is on the line. A poor outfielder will hurt a team sooner or later.

The busiest outfielder is the center fielder. But that doesn't mean center is the hardest place to play. All three positions have some tough points. But the center fielder must be very fast. He has to cover the most ground by far.

In most cases, the rule is that the center fielder takes any ball he can reach. He must be able to come in on short flies to either side of him, and go back on balls hit over his head. This is very hard. He must also be able to get balls hit to his right or left. These spots are called the outfield gaps. The center fielder must make an instant judgment on these balls. Because if he misplays them and the ball gets past him, the batter might get a triple or even a home run.

The right and left fielders don't have to run as far. The fences are usually closer in right and left, and they have the foul line to one side. Still, they must learn to play the corners, where the foul line meets the outfield fence. Balls hit hard into the corners often bounce out at strange angles. If the right and left fielders don't know about this, the ball can bounce right past them. Then they have trouble.

There are several things that all three outfielders must do well. All must be able to throw, though as a rule the center and right fielder usually have the stronger arms. They have longer throws to make. Sometimes the center fielder has to throw from the deepest part of the ball park. And the right fielder often has to throw all the way to third or to home. Outfield throws must be made on a straight line so they get there fast. Sometimes an outfielder will throw on one bounce to a base. There is nothing wrong with this. It's better than a high, lazy throw that takes all day to get there.

The outfielders must also be able to charge ground ball base hits and pick them up quickly. If they don't, a fast base runner will take an extra base. They must also work together. When a ball is hit between them, one must shout, "I've got it!" so that the other gets out of the way. There have been times when two outfielders have collided and serious injuries have resulted. Outfielders have also been hurt running into the walls and fences. However, many of today's parks have thick padding on the walls to protect the fielders.

Outfielders must also back each other up. If a ball is hit to left, the center fielder can't relax and watch the play. He must race over as fast as he can in case the left fielder misses it or it gets past him. Then he can back him up and perhaps keep the runner from taking an extra base.

The outfielders must also know the hitters. That means knowing where a hitter usually hits the ball so he can move over in that direction when the hitter comes up. The manager, catcher, and infielders sometimes help move the outfielders around. They must also watch the wind and sun, us-

ing their sunglasses when they have to. So there is much more to playing the outfield than just catching a nice high fly every now and then.

One more short word about fielding. Each baseball field is different, whether it be Little League, college, the minors, or the big leagues. There are things players must watch out for in one park that do not exist in another. For instance, the left field fence may not be padded in one stadium and fully padded in another. So the fielder may be a bit more daring in the padded park because he knows he won't get hurt hitting the fence.

The point is that a good player must know all these things. He must always look around and learn about each place. He must also know if there are any special rules for that stadium. These are called ground rules. The umpires remind the managers of the ground rules before a game, and the managers tell the players.

An example of this is the ground rule double. This rule is the same in all major league parks. If a fly ball is hit fair to the outfield and bounces into the stands, the batter automaticaly has a double. If he has stopped at first, he may go to second. Or if he has already rounded second, he must stop and go back. That is a special rule to cover a special kind of play. All the players must know these rules. It's part of becoming a good ballplayer.

Mickey Rivers backs up his Yankee teammate Lou Piniella, who has called for the ball.

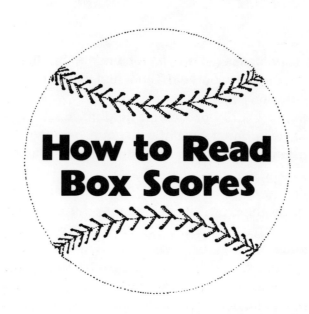

How to Read Box Scores

At the end of newspaper stories about baseball games, you usually find the names of the players in the game. After each name are numbers and letters. And there is more information right below. These lists are called box scores. Below is the box score of the final game of the 1977 World Series. It was played October 18, 1977, between the New York Yankees and Los Angeles Dodgers.

LOS ANGELES (N)	AB.	R.	H.	RBI.
Lopes, 2b	4	0	1	0
Russell, ss	3	0	0	0
Smith, rf	4	2	1	1
Cey, 3b	3	1	1	0
Garvey, 1b	4	1	2	2
Baker, lf	4	0	1	0
Monday, cf	4	0	1	0
Yeager, c	3	0	1	0
Davalillo, ph	1	0	1	1
Hooton, p	2	0	0	0
Sosa, p	0	0	0	0
Rau, p	0	0	0	0
Goodson, ph	1	0	0	0
Hough, p	0	0	0	0
Lacy, ph	1	0	0	0
Total	34	4	9	4

YANKEES (A)	AB.	R.	H.	RBI.
Rivers, cf	4	0	2	0
Randolph, 2b	4	1	0	0
Munson, c	4	1	1	0
Jackson, rf	3	4	3	5
Chambliss, 1b	4	2	2	2
Nettles, 3b	4	0	0	0
Piniella, lf	3	0	0	1
Dent, ss	2	0	0	0
Torrez, p	3	0	0	0
Total	31	8	8	8

Los Angeles .... 2 0 1   0 0 0   0 0 1—4
Yankees .... 0 2 0   3 2 0   0 1 x—8
　Error—Dent. Double plays—Yankees 2. Left on base—Los Angeles 5, Yankees 2. Two base hit—Chambliss. Three base hit—Garvey. Home runs—Chambliss (1), Smith (3), Jackson 3 (5). Sacrifice fly—Piniella.

	IP.	H.	R.	ER	BB	SO
Hooton (L, 1-1)	3	3	4	4	1	1
Sosa	1⅔	3	3	3	1	0
Rau	1⅓	0	0	0	0	1
Hough	2	2	1	1	0	2
Torrez (W, 2-0)	9	9	4	2	2	6

　Passed ball—Munson. Time of game—2:19. Attendance—56,407.

The letters right after a player's name stand for the position he plays. The letter c is for catcher, p is for pitcher, 1b is for first baseman, cf is for center fielder, and so on. The visiting team is always on the left side of the box score and the home team on the right. By the way, the ph stands for pinch hitter.

　The letters above each column of numbers show what the numbers mean. The letters AB stand for the number of times in the game each player was at bat. Since a walk, a sacrifice hit, and being hit with a pitch don't count as a time at bat, they are not shown under AB. In other words, if a player grounds out, singles, walks, and strikes out, the number 3 will appear next to the player's name under AB.

　The letter R means the number of times a player has scored during the game: in other words, the number of times he has safely crossed home plate. The H stands for the number of hits the players made during the game and includes singles, doubles, triples, and home runs.

　The final letters at the top, RBI, stand for the number of runs batted in a player has made. A player gets a run batted in when a hit, sacrifice fly, squeeze bunt, or other method causes a run to cross the plate. If the bases are loaded and a player hits a single, allowing two runs to score, he has two RBIs. If he walks with the bases loaded, forcing home a run, he gets one RBI. If he hits a homer with the bases loaded, he gets four RBIs, since he has also caused himself to cross the plate by hitting the home run.

At the bottom of these four columns are the team totals for the entire game. Under that comes the line score, showing in what inning each team scored its runs. The X in the Yankees' column in the ninth inning shows that the Yanks didn't have to bat that inning. If the home team is ahead when the visitors are out in the ninth, the game is over.

Below the line score is some additional information about the game. It shows that there was one error in the game. It was made by Yankee shortstop Bucky Dent. Next it shows that the Yanks made two double plays. Some box scores tell which players made the double plays. Then it tells how many runners were left on base by each team. These are runners who are still on base when the third out is made. They have not scored.

Next it shows there was one double in the game, by Chris Chambliss. There was one triple, or three-base hit, by Steve Garvey. And there were five home runs. Chambliss hit one, Reggie Smith hit one, and Reggie Jackson hit three. The numbers in parentheses show how many total homers they've hit in the series. And the final information shows a sacrifice fly by Piniella.

Some box scores do not spell these things out. They use symbols. In the same order they would be E for error, DP for double plays, LOB for left on base, 2B for doubles, 3B for triples, HR for home runs, and SF for sacrifice fly.

Next come the pitching records. They show which pitcher won and lost the game. In parentheses are the pitching records for the series. During the regular season it would show the season records. Next come innings pitched. If a pitcher goes 1⅓ innings it means he pitched one full inning, but only got one man out in the next inning. Each out makes one-third of an inning on a pitcher's record. A starting pitcher must pitch at least five full innings to get a win. If he leaves the game sooner, for whatever reason, he cannot win. A reliever can win any time his team scores the winning run while he's pitching, even if he only pitches an inning.

After innings pitched (IP) come hits (H). This shows how many hits the pitcher has given up. After that comes the runs (R) scored while the pitcher was in there, and then the earned runs (ER) scored off the pitcher. An earned run is one that has been scored without an error. If the team makes an error to let a run score, it is not the pitcher's fault. So it is not an earned run against his record. An earned-run average shows how many earned runs a pitcher gives up per nine innings pitched. So if his earned-run average is 2.75, it means that pitcher gives up 2.75 runs per nine-inning game.

The final two columns show the number of walks or bases on balls (BB) and strikeouts (SO) that the pitcher has gotten during the game.

And finally the box score shows a passed ball by Munson. A passed ball is a ball that gets past the catcher. The official scorer rules that he should have caught it. It's almost like an error. Then comes the time of the game and the number of people who were there—the attendance. Some box scores also list the names of the umpires.

Much of the information in the box score can be found in the game story. But the box score is a summary of the entire game and you can tell quite a bit about the game by just reading it.

Organized Baseball

Millions of Americans of all ages play baseball just for the fun of it. Go to any park or open field during the warm weather and it's a good bet there will be some people playing ball. Whether it's youngsters of ten or men of fifty, if they are playing for fun, they are called amateurs. Even youngsters in Little Leagues and men in local city leagues are amateurs. That's because they don't get paid for playing.

Then there is a group of men who do get paid to play baseball. In fact, they play baseball for a living. It's their job and they work at it from March to October every year. These men are called professionals, or pros.

At the top of the professional ladder are the major leagues, or big leagues. This is where all professional players want to play. But they can't always get there right away. Sometimes they must play in lesser professional leagues called the minor leagues. Players can't make much money in the minor leagues, so they all work hard to reach the majors.

Yet each league works the same way. Teams are grouped together in divisions of maybe six, eight, or ten teams. At the end of the year the team with the best record wins that division. Then that team will usually play a team from another division for the championship of that league. That's what everyone shoots for all year.

The major leagues consist of two separate leagues, the National and American. As of 1978, there were twelve teams in the National League and fourteen in the American League. Each league is divided into two divisions, east and west. At the end of the season, which is 162 games long, the teams with the best record in each division of each league play each other. The first team to win three games wins the league pennant. It then meets the pennant winner from the other league in the World Series. The World Series is a best four of seven series and is one of the great spectacles in all of sports. Millions and millions of people watch on television to see which team will be World Champion.

There are several levels of minor leagues. The highest level is called Triple A (AAA). Then come Double A (AA) and A leagues. Below that are the low minors, starting with rookie and instructional leagues. When a big-league team picks a player from a college or high school, it sees how good he is. Then the parent club places him in the minor league with the same kind of players. As he gets better, he is moved up to the higher minors until he is ready for the majors. Some players take years to get to the majors. Some never make it at all. So it's not always an easy road to the big time.

Like all the other major sports, baseball today is a big business. There are many people working for each major league team. And each major league team is connected with a number of minor league teams. When it places a player

**Yankee outfielder Lou Piniella
climbs the wall in an attempt
to catch a home run ball.**

there, no other major league team can move in and take him, unless it is done legally and as a business deal.

The teams also spend a lot of money on managers and coaches to teach these minor league players how to become better at the game. They also have men called scouts who spend a great deal of time looking at young ballplayers all over the country. They are looking for players they think will make it to the big leagues. If they sign a player, he usually begins his pro career in the minor leagues.

The season begins in March of each year when all the big-league teams go to a warm climate for spring training. There are many players at spring training, all of them fighting for a job with the major league club. It is up to the manager and coaches to pick the players who will stay in the majors. The others are sent to the various minor league teams. Sometimes a player can be called up from the minors to the majors in the middle of the season. This is usually done to replace another player who is hurt or a player in the majors who is not doing well.

As with all good athletes, the baseball player should take very good care of his body. He must always be in top shape, eat right, and get the right amount of rest. That way, he will play better and there is less chance of his getting hurt. Most athletes know what is best for them and it is up to them to take care of themselves. No one can do it for them.

For many years, baseball was a sport for boys and men only. Today, many girls and women are enjoying the game, too. Some have their own leagues, and a few girls have been playing with the boys at the Little League level. All this proves that baseball is more popular than ever before. It is an American game that has been played for more than one hundred years now. It is truly our national pastime.

Index